Perfectly
Imperfect

*Inspirational Stories
of Gratitude,
Kindness & Family*

Dawn Ruggie

Perfectly Imperfect
Copyright © 2022 by Dawn Ruggie
ISBN: 978-1-7374876-1-6

All rights reserved.
Printed in the United States

No part of this book may be used or reproduced in any manner whatsoever without the written permission of the author except in the case of brief quotations embodied in critical articles and reviews.

The events told in this book are the author's memories of events. Some names have been changed to protect the privacy of the people involved.

Cover design by https://sweetnspicydesigns.com/

Published by
DRI Publications
Red Hill, PA
DawnRuggieInspires.com

I dedicate this book to my Uncle George. The strongest man I have known and such a kind soul. He will forever be missed.

Table of Contents

Introduction 1

Forgiveness
Chapter 1: My Bio Dad 5
Chapter 2: My Bio Mom 9
Chapter 3: About Forgiveness 11

Gratitude
Chapter 4: Uncle George 16
Chapter 5: About Gratitude 23

Acceptance
Chapter 6: Foster Care 28
Chapter 7: About Acceptance 33

Life's Whispers
Chapter 8: My Beautiful Brie 38
Chapter 9: About Life's Whispers 45

The Third Law of Motion
Chapter 10: Candace 51
Chapter 11: About The Third Law of Motion 56

Kindness
Chapter 12: Francesca 61
Chapter 13: About Kindness 66

Failure

Chapter 14: Family Visit 71
Chapter 15: About Failure 76

Service

Chapter 16: Claire 81
Chapter 17: Isabella 85
Chapter 18: About Service 87

Conclusion

Chapter 19: Grow With Me 91

Acknowledgements 94
About the Author 95

"If you have been brutally broken but still have the courage to be gentle to other living beings, then you're a badass with a heart of an angel."

-Keanu Reeves

"Remember you were given this life because you are strong enough to live it."

-Unknown

Introduction

There is nothing wrong with having more than one mom and dad, It only means more people to share the love with.

My name is Dawn. I was born in Pennsylvania in 1976 to two wild and adventurous teens who did not have a good support system. My biological father battled mental illness and addiction. My biological mother was kicked out of her home when her mom found out she was pregnant.

When I was two years old I began living with my father's sister, Marylou, and my paternal grandmother. After a few short years my grandmother passed away. Marylou, who I now call mom, continued to raise me and later married a man named Bill.

When I started school, kids would always ask me why I didn't have parents. This got to be quite annoying. I just wanted to go to school, learn, and play during recess. I didn't want to answer a bunch of questions about my life.

One day I came home from school and asked my aunt if I could call her mom. I remember being in the kitchen with her and standing near the stove when I asked the question.

"Of course," she replied.

"Thank you. The kids at school keep asking me why I don't have a mom."

She gave me a big hug and I knew from that day on everything would be okay. I met many challenges being raised under these circumstances, but I do not reflect on them in a negative way.

I still have a relationship with my biological mother; her not raising me does not lessen her role in my life. My biological father moved away when I was eight. From that point on, I had limited contact with him until his passing.

It seemed from the start that my life was going to be one worth sharing. It took me a long time to be comfortable telling others about my family dynamics because my opinion has not always been the same as everyone around me, and I have learned that "different," means "bad" to some people. I now understand that my opinion is based on my experiences while other people's opinions are based on their experiences. Our opinions couldn't possibly be the same as our experiences are too different.

In my thirties I realized it would be a great idea to have a book written about my journey but never knew how it would happen. It took me until my forty-fourth year to realize I had the ability to share it myself.

There have been many events in my life that have shaped me into the person I am today. I have been given a wonderful ability to find the good in any situation. It doesn't mean the bad didn't happen; it just means I will ensure something good comes out every experience, something to better myself or the lives of the people around me.

I am going to share with you some of the events that have had an impact on my life and the lessons I have taken away from them. Some experiences are subtle, and some are traumatic but they have all had a part in who I am today and the choices I make.

Forgiveness

Chapter 1
My Bio Dad

The year was 1975, the town was Fairless Hills, and two teens were in love. Well, they believed it was love. At 16 I'm not sure if it's love or infatuation but they couldn't go without seeing each other. They would even sneak out for late night rendezvous. My biological dad would climb out the window and head across the street over to the small, one floor home with three girls and one boy. He'd go to the girls' bedroom window.

Tap, tap. "Barb"

Tap, tap. "Barb, you awake?"

"Yes. I'm awake. I'll be right out."

And that's where I come into the picture.

Nine months later on a hot summer day at dawn I was born. The name they had originally picked for me was Adonica Dawn but at the hospital they decided to change it to Dawn Marie. It must have been the only year that name was popular because every Dawn I have ever met is my age.

None of the above details really matter, though. The most

important thing was that I came into this world being loved, and every day after that, all I remember are the people around me showing me how much they loved me. Maybe it was because I was not an expected pregnancy or maybe it was because my parents were absent often.

My mother and father did try to do things right. In April of 1976 at the young age of 17, and while my mom was six months pregnant, they got married. On the ride to the church with the windows down they played the song "Chapel of Love" by The Dixie Cups. Close family and friends gathered to celebrate the occasion. It seemed as though everything was going good for them, right? Well, it wasn't.

My grandmother kicked my mom out of the house when she found out Mom was pregnant. My father was wild and hard to control. And they had no money. My mother really didn't have clothes that fit her because of her growing belly. I have no idea if either one of them worked at this time but I am assuming they did not.

I lived with them until I was about two years old. I can only imagine I was not with them all the time. I know my aunt, who raised me and became my mom, had me a lot of the time, even before I officially lived with her.

Of course, how I ended up with my Aunt Marylou has multiple sides to the story and I'm sure the truth lies somewhere in the middle. Was I picked up less and less until I eventually wasn't picked up? Was I left there more and more because of the abuse my dad dished out on my mom? Or was it because they were selfish and I became an inconvenience to their lifestyle?

I had occasional in-person contact with my biological father until I was about eight years old. I remember him living at my aunt's house when I was very young and then eventually he got his own place. I would go to the apartment he shared with his girlfriend for a couple of hours. I never remember sleeping there but I may have.

I remember his uncontrollable outbursts. There are two particularly that stand out in my memories. I remember him going up and down the hallway at our apartment screaming and yelling. I also remember him cutting his hand and I remember the blood. I was taken to a neighbor's house until it was safe for me to come back home. The second time I was in the bedroom of his apartment with my dad, his girlfriend, and her children. Something was said that really upset him and he started yelling. His girlfriend came up to me, took me by the hand and said, "Dawn, I want you to stay under this table by the wall and don't come out until I get you."

I sat there listening to furniture being thrown, glass shattering, cries, and profanities being shouted back and forth by each of them. When the storm was over his girlfriend came back and said, "Dawn, you can come out now. I am going to call your mom to come get you and take you home."

By this time I was calling my aunt "mom," and that is who she was referring to. I have no idea how long the event took place but it did not seem like an extremely long time. That could be a coping mechanism I created within myself to help me get through it.

When I was eight years old my dad's temper got him into big trouble. He was forced to quickly move out of the state. I did not see him again until I was twenty-one years old. In one swift move he was gone. Once he got settled he would call every once in a while. I looked forward to the calls but I was the only one who did. When he would call, I believe it

triggered my family's emotions, and I don't blame them.
 They would tell me the reasons I shouldn't talk to him or remind me of the kind of person he was. I didn't need the reminders. I knew he was an alcoholic, and I knew he talked mostly bull crap but I still wanted to stay connected to him. I just needed them to remember that he was my biological father and that I knew everything about him, but I still missed him.
 I never wanted them to share my feelings with others. Not having the support I was looking for left me feeling as if I had no one to talk to about my loss.
 In 2009, my family received a call from the California Coroner's office stating that my biological father had committed suicide. When my family told me about his passing, I could tell they wanted to support me but since I felt alone in this area of my life I could not accept that support. I kept my feelings private. I had lots of emotions but mostly knew he was finally at peace. His demons ravaged both him and his loved ones his entire life. When I went to California to make the final arrangements I was told that he was diagnosed with paranoid schizophrenia and that he refused treatment and eventually succumbed to his demons.
 When I look back on my time with him it will always be of me sitting high on his broad shoulders, listening to Elvis, and the sound of his deep voice telling me his fantasy stories. Even though I had heard him use his voice as a weapon in many situations there was something calming about it. Maybe because he was just an injured soul violently spilling out his hurt on others.

Chapter 2
My Bio Mom

It was evening; the sky was dark and the inside of our house was warm with lights. I was eleven. I cleaned my room in anticipation of her coming. Now I paced back and forth peering out the window looking for my bio mom's car. I didn't even know what she drove, but I still looked for a car to pull into our driveway.

Knock, knock.

I quickly swung open the door and said "Hello" with a big smile.

She replied, "Hello."

We talked and I showed her around the house. The tension was very high, but we naturally clicked. That night after she left, I laid my head down on the pillow. I felt a sense of calm and overwhelming excitement.

That weekend I received a call. "Dawn, it's Barb. Would you like to go out to breakfast with me?"

"Yes! I'd love to." Holy cow, was I nervous! What would we talk about? Should I be scared? Then I reminded myself that this was so exciting. I was finally getting to spend time with my mom. A short time later she picked me up. We went to a small diner and talked about everything under the sun. It was something I had looked forward to for such a long time, especially since the absence of my biological father.

As time went on we grew closer and closer. I realized we had a lot in common even though we had not spent time together.

My love for my biological mom does not take from the love I have for my parents and the other family members who had a hand in raising me and I never want them to feel as if it does. I can only imagine it has been hard for them.

The things from my childhood that I have juggled around in my mind are good part of my life. They have had a huge impact on the way I parent and love my children. This happened without me even realizing it. I did not see it until I started my own healing journey. After a long time of processing through the emotions I realized we are all people who have been through things and are healing from the things we have been through.

Chapter 3
About Forgiveness

What if forgiveness has nothing to do with the other person? This lesson is one which I had to learn over and over again until I finally got it.

Anger and resentment can be like a thief in the night. You have no idea the hold they have on you until many years later. I have come to realize that forgiveness is only about our own feelings and our own personal growth, not others.

Merriam-Webster.com's definition of forgive is "to cease to feel resentment against (an offender)." This supports my theory. This definition says nothing about the other person's act being viewed as acceptable behavior or whether or not you think the behavior was wrong. It only speaks of one's own feelings of resentment.

Forgiving doesn't condone the person's actions, it's just a way to release the grip it has on you. A long period of time can go by and you forget what you were angry about. Then something happens that triggers that part of you. The anger and the rage can come out on an innocent person who just happened to push the right button at the wrong time.

Once I realized all I had to do was acknowledge the thing that had hurt me, and how it affected me, I could release it from my worry—and my life started to change. I saw things from a whole new perspective.

It is not my responsibility to help others see how their actions affect people. That is a lesson each person needs to learn for themselves in their own time. I cannot wait until the person who has hurt me has finished learning their own lessons until I forgive them and become free of the burden of my anger and resentment.

I am sure the things that happened in my early years were not intentional. My bio mom and dad did not mean to hurt me. Some of my memories used to bring up less desirable emotions for me, but only because I didn't understand why they had acted in certain way. As I matured, I realized how different my experiences are from the other people who are experiencing an event—any event. Even though we are doing the same thing at the same time, our needs and expectations of each other are different.

Even though things in my childhood caused me pain I needed to let it go. We were not in a position of mutual understanding and most likely never will be. That doesn't mean we can't have a good relationship. I just have to take control of my actions and limit the topics I engage in.

Unfortunately, there are times when the hurt and pain is so much that you need to cut off contact with that person. I have learned that's okay too. Sometimes you cross each other's path later in life and things end up better than they would have been if you had kept in contact.

There are some things in life that we are meant to do

alone. Forgiveness is one of them. If a person comes to you at some point and offers an apology and asks to make things right, that is wonderful, but you can't hold yourself back from your life's purpose because of someone else's wrongdoing. There are so many adventures to be had, so many people to meet, and if you hold onto that anger it will undoubtedly prevent some of these things from happening.

I encourage you to do the things needed to keep your vibration high so you can go out into the world being the best version of yourself prepared for what life has to offer you.

 *When you forgive you don't change the past…you change the future.*

Author Unknown

Gratitude

Chapter 4
Uncle George

    The year was 1990. I was a teenager and life was good. I grew up living next door to my aunt and uncle who I loved. They were always busy, worked hard, and loved camping. I never realized the impact they would have on my life until I no longer had one of them. Sometimes it takes a great loss to realize the strength we have buried within.

    After school I would come home, watch cartoons, then lie in my bed. Around 6 p.m. I would wait to hear my aunt and uncle's cars drive up the street. I'd lie there patiently as I listened for them to pull into their driveway and hear the car doors open and then the bang of them closing. I would allow a few minutes to pass for them to get settled in the house before I hopped out of my bed, ran out of my room, out the front door, and toward the chain link fence in between our yards. As I approached the fence I would place my hands on the top of it, bracing myself as I hopped right over into their yard. This only lasted a few more years because around 1993 my Uncle George worked his last day. It must have been so difficult for him to accept. He was only in his late 30s when he became too sick to continue his career as a radiology technician.

He was one of a kind. So funny and so full of life. It was impossible not to like him. He was also the strongest person I ever met. He lived a lifetime with a debilitating disease called Cystic Fibrosis. I never once heard him complain. He took full advantage of the time he had here. He woke up each day and made the decision to have a great day.

When he was diagnosed at only six months old, his life expectancy was only a few years. So many times in his life the doctors would say, "He won't live to start school," or "He won't live long enough to go to high school." He was told he would never marry, never have kids, never go to college…well he proved them wrong in every way. He graduated high school, became a radiology tech, and married a woman who had a son whom he later adopted and raised as his own.

I never saw anger in him over the limits that were put on him. He just always lived knowing that only God knows when our time will be done, and no one knows what strengths we hold within ourselves.

Each evening when I would get to their house, he would usually be sitting at the table filling up his shot glass with his daily medications. I'd walk around talking about whatever event was going on in my life at the time. As he watched me he said "Dawn, can you get me a drink?" Still talking I opened the cabinet, grabbed out a class and poured him a cup of tea. I had to be careful where I placed things because all his nebulizer equipment was laid out on the counter drying. Each time it was used it was cleaned meticulously so there was never a chance for infection. "Here you go." I said as I handed it to him. He took it, picked up the shot glass and downed the pills like it was a shot of whisky. I can't even imagine how he did it.

    He would then get up and walk over to his chair. As I followed, I always stopped by the candy dispenser and treated myself to a delicious, multi-colored, chocolate-filled, button-sized candy. The never-ending line of oxygen tubing zig-zagged all across the room. I carefully stepped over it each time as though it was his lifeline. I knew If I stepped on it nothing would happen, but at that age I didn't really understand it and wanted to make sure I did nothing to hurt him.

    As the years passed, he went out less and you could tell the disease was getting the better of him, but his light still shone brightly. He laughed, told jokes, and played pranks on my aunt. My favorite was when he would put on his werewolf mask and hide around Halloween. He would jump out from the dark and she'd scream a high-pitched scream as if this never happened to her before.

    When I graduated high school and moved out on my own, I still made sure I went there each week to spend time with him. This is also the time I started having dreams of my uncle. They were relentless. I'd go to sleep and dream that I was outside my aunt and uncle's home. I would enter the front door and go straight to the candy dispenser. My uncle would say, "Can I have a kiss?" I didn't like to give my uncle a kiss. I looked down at my hand and there was a chocolate kiss from the dispenser. I handed it to him and the dream would abruptly end.

    February 1996, at 19, I gave birth to my first son. I was

so in love with him and couldn't wait to share him with all my loved ones. Unfortunately, Uncle George was unable to be around my son for six weeks to three months due to a bacteria my uncle carried.

This was also at a time when my uncle really needed some joy brought to him. He was almost always at home. His days consisted of visits from medical staff, therapies, and hospital stays. Life was moving forward and somehow it was happening without him. Still, he never complained, he always greeted everyone with his smile.

A few weeks into February I was visiting my parents who still lived next door to my aunt and uncle. I had my son with me, so I bundled him up really well. It didn't feel quite as cold as other days earlier in the month. I called my uncle.

"Hello," he answered in his deep, raspy voice. I could hear the sound of the oxygen through the phone as I waited for him to take a breath so he could answer the next question.

"Hey Uncle George! Can you go to the kitchen window? I have something to show you."

"Ok. Give me a minute," he replied.

I quickly went over to his yard, because I knew once he got to the window he might be too weak to stand long. As he approached the window, he looked out at me and saw my infant son all bundled up in my arms. I made sure my son's face clearly showed in his blankets as I held him close to the window. My uncle's smile was so big and bright it lit the world. It absolutely made his day. I did this several times until they were cleared to be around each other.

My son Michael became a big part of his joy. He loved it when I visited with Michael. "Michael, come sit on the chair with me. We can watch some TV shows together." Michael ran right over and hopped on his lap. While he sat there I'd watch Michael feeding him licorice and them both sipping on their cups and then letting out a big sigh afterwards. Until this day if I hear that sound it takes me back to those wonderful memories.

Due to his Cystic Fibrosis, Uncle George always had to have a small cup by him. People with this disease overproduce mucus and need to constantly expel it from their lungs. Michael quickly learned that was something he couldn't touch. The bond between the sick and the young is so beautiful. It's an unspoken knowledge that they both have something to offer one another.

In July 1997, my uncle took a turn for the worse. He was rushed to the hospital. I prayed they would help him and we would be back to our regular visits. This time was different though. He was losing strength and the disease was getting the better of him. After some time in the hospital, he made the decision to come home to pass away surrounded by his family and friends. Late in the evening transport was set up, medical equipment was delivered to the home, and the downstairs bedroom was transformed into an at-home hospital room.

That weekend there was a block party on the street. The music was blasting, and everyone was laughing. The vibrant sounds could be heard from inside his room even though the windows were closed, air conditioning was on, and several fans were continuously blowing on him. It didn't take long for everyone at the block party to realize how grave my uncle's condition had become. They brought the party to him.

One by one they came in with their larger-than-life personalities and embraced him. They shared some of their favorite memories with him and let him know how much he was loved. It's so wonderful to know he left this world the same ways he lived it.

I was working the night he passed. I called to check in on him before my shift ended. I had to be in in the morning and wasn't sure if I should stop to see him then or in the morning before work. My mom answered the phone. "Hello," I said. "How is Uncle George?"

"He is good right now. He's sitting in his chair eating a bowl of cereal."

I knew he would be tired after that, so I decided to go home and let him get some sleep. I asked her to tell him I loved him, and the conversation ended.

I got home, showered, got ready for bed, and quickly fell asleep. A short time later, my phone rang. My heart sank. With a lump in my throat, I answered the phone and heard one of my family members.

"Hi Dawn, Uncle George just passed away. We are still at the house. You can come see him if you would like."

I hung up the phone, and in a panic got on my clothes. My entire body was shaking, I was nauseous and so mad at myself for not going there after work. If only I had known!

When I arrived and saw him, he looked so peaceful. The struggle was finally over. I walked over to him and sat with him for some time. When it was time to leave I stood up, walked up to him and I gently placed a kiss on his forehead "Uncle George I love you so much. I will never forget you. Thank you for all the lessons you have taught me." My relentless dream had prepared me for this moment.

I knew I had to give him a kiss. Since that day I have

never had that dream again. I had a feeling the time was coming close because the dreams were coming more often and with so much detail. Handing him the chocolate kiss would repeat over and over again. That was the moment my body was telling me to focus on. I had to give him a kiss for my own closure. I didn't want to walk away with any regrets.

Chapter 5
About Gratitude

During some of the darkest days of my life I've searched for many ways to lift myself up. I've tried almost everything but it was one of the simplest things that put me back on the path to happiness. Oftentimes people would tell me the more you're grateful, the more you will find to be grateful for but that is hard to see when your mind is telling you every negative reason to hate life.

I assumed I had to wait until I got my mind under control before I could start practicing gratitude. I figured I was too deep and that was too simple of a solution to save me from the depths of my depression.

When I felt I had exhausted all other options I decided to give it a try. I started by waking up every morning and telling myself five things I was grateful for. It could be the simplest of things, the fact that I woke up, the sun, the temperature outside, that I had a job.

At first it seemed very difficult to find reasons to be grateful even though I knew I had many good things in my life. My mind had taken control of me, and I believed everything it told me. As time went on the five items came to me more quickly and before I knew it the things that were hard for me to see were jumping right out at me and they were things that had so much more meaning in life.

This practice slowly progressed throughout the day. When my mind would creep up and try to take over, I naturally started to think of things that I was grateful for in the negative situation that was playing in my head. For example, when my dad had his stroke there were many reasons to be upset. There were many reasons to be angry at life. He went from working two jobs to being in a rehab center and then getting therapy at home. I would remind myself how many times my parents had come to stay at our house since his stroke, time that we did not spend together before because he and my mom worked so much. That is time my kids and I love and appreciate.

It started happening without me even making the conscious decision to do it. My body was picking up on what I was doing and started to do it automatically. It became easier and easier, and once my body started doing it automatically the negative thoughts did not stay with me as long.

Before gratitude I could sit with a single negative thought for days, weeks, sometimes even longer. It was awful. It still amazes me that something so simple could have such a profound effect on one's life.

I never remember my Uncle George telling me he practiced gratitude but I have no doubt he did. I can't even say if he knew he did, but I know he always had a positive outlook on any situation, and I never heard him complain and he had so many more valid reasons to be mad at life. If he could overcome his thoughts and live his best life I have no doubt I can, and so can you.

The first step I took for this change was just making the decision to start doing the work. I know it may seem hard at first but struggling is hard, too. You just have to decide which hard you are going to accept into your life. I chose to do the work because I had faith that if I do it life would eventually get better. I felt deep inside me that if I didn't make that choice things would always be difficult, and I would never get to the point of enjoying life again.

For me, there was nothing that I did to contribute to my trauma, but I knew it was my responsibility to heal from my traumatic experiences. If I didn't, life would just snowball into more pain for me and for the people around me. When I was hurting, I am sure I was not the most pleasant person to be around and that transferred into how I treated others and then how they felt and then how they treated others, and so on.

Once the first step has been taken, each step gets easier and easier and before you know it, you are in a completely different place looking back at the huge staircase you climbed with pride. You had no idea how you could do it, but realize you did what you once believed was impossible.

 *"Gratitude unlocks the fullness of life. It turns what we have into enough, and more."*

-Melody Beattie

Acceptance

Chapter 6

Foster Care

It was a fall evening; the leaves were so colorful they painted the lawns in orange and yellow and gold as I walked up the street to our mailbox. On my way back I opened the one envelope from the foster care agency. It was our foster parent cards. I jumped up and down in the middle of the road, leaves crunching with every jump.

I called my husband Matt on the phone. "Guess what?" I didn't even give him a chance to answer. "We're officially foster parents. Our cards came." He was just as happy as I was.

I couldn't stay home alone. I was full of too much excitement. I decided to take a drive over to my best friend Becky's house. She was right around the corner.

Becky was home with her husband making dinner when I arrived. The aroma in the kitchen was mouthwatering. I sat down at the kitchen island so excited. I had mentioned about becoming foster parents to her previously, but I was not sure if she knew how serious we were about it.

I could barely contain myself as I pulled out my card and set it on the counter. She looked at it and said, "What's this?"

"My foster parent card." I replied. She set it down rather quickly, shook her head and then turned away with a sigh. I asked, "What's wrong?"

"You guys are really going to do this?"

"Yes."

"Why not just have more kids?"

"That's not why we are doing this. We want to give a home to a child in need."

"Welp, Nothing good can come from foster care."

"Really Becky? I don't agree. I think only good can come from foster care."

I knew this conversation was not headed in a good direction, so I decided to gather my stuff. "Becky, Matt will be home from work shortly, so I am going to have to get going. I just wanted to stop by and show you my card. I'll talk to you soon."

"Okay, I'll see you at work."

I went home and shared my experience with Matt. He wasn't surprised by Becky's reaction and told me not to pay any attention to it, but it really bothered me. The kids in the foster care system are just innocent bystanders to adults around them. They are not the ones who initiated these decisions.

Over the next couple months while we were waiting to be placed with a child I did not talk to Becky about it much. Once in a while I would give her updates but it was very limited. When we got the call to be placed with a set of twins I couldn't wait to share the news with everyone, even with my best friend Becky. I had hoped that she had had enough time to adjust to our decision and maybe do some research of her own.

I invited her and her husband over for dinner to share our

news. I made salad, spaghetti, meatballs, and Italian bread. She brought dessert and wine. We sat down and ate, cleaned up and I planned on breaking the news during dessert.

Just as we all sat back down at the table and were cutting the cake and serving wine, I made the announcement.

"I have some news! We received a call and we are possibly going to be placed with a set of twins. One boy and one girl."

Right away Becky answered, "Are you sure about this. I have been thinking and I have so many concerns."

"Yes. We are prepared for them. I already have all the baby supplies I need."

"What do you know about the family? They could be drug addicts?"

"They could be but there are systems in place to keep everyone safe. I am not going to worry about that unless it is an issue. I don't even know their circumstances yet."

"Are they white?"

"No."

"Why wouldn't you tell them white children? They are not going to look like your children at all and people will be looking at you, especially the boy. What are your neighbors going to think? You know nothing about their culture. You're not going to be any better parents for them."

"We are doing this to help a child in need not to be placed with a child that looks like us. And as far as race, yes, we will have a lot to learn but we are capable of learning everything we need to know and we will reach out to our community and friends when needed."

"I just don't understand. They could bring drugs into the house. They could have mental illness."

"They are babies. They won't be bringing drugs in and my family history has addiction and mental health problems so they won't be any different from the rest of us."

"But you beat it so your kids will be fine."

"You don't beat mental illness. You either have it or you don't. One may not even show signs of it until later in life. Anyone can be diagnosed with mental illness."

This was not at all what I expected from my friend. I knew there might be some resistance but I had never experienced anything like this before. I was in total shock. I really didn't know how to handle the situation. I expected her to be understanding of my answers but her position on the situation was so strong there was no changing her mind.

That night changed our relationship. I expected her to react the way I would have but that only left me feeling disappointed. I have no harsh feelings for her I just have an understanding that in some ways we are different and it's a difference I can not control.

This was the first of many heartbreaking experiences I had while raising children of different races. This was hard for me to understand at first, but I later realized to be a good parent to children of other races I needed to experience it firsthand. I learned Becky did not stand alone.

This experience was too prominent in this journey not to be a lesson I needed to learn. Plus, it kept happening over and over again. After many tears and sleepless nights, I realized I had to experience it myself so I could properly teach my children how to handle it. Not just the children I fostered but also my biological children. The environment I was raised in never exposed me to anything like it. Once I realized this I was able to move into the acceptance stage of my journey.

Our home is very diverse and I wouldn't have it any other way. We have experienced so many different cultures, foods, and traditions. My children are better human beings because of this. They see no color or social status. If they feel you are a good person they will welcome you with open arms. I just adore watching them interacting with others.

Chapter 7
About Acceptance

    Everyone has their own purpose to fulfill in this journey we call life. We all have our own path to follow, and many lessons will be learned. People come and go to help us see the lessons and at times to redirect us. It can be hard to accept when someone suddenly changes their path, especially if it's not in the same direction as the one we are already traveling. Of course we want to bring the ones closest to us on our journey but it may not be the one for them.
    We all have had experiences that have led us to the destination we are currently residing in. Accepting the other person's journey does not mean you accept their behaviors; it just means you acknowledge they are heading in a different direction than you and you have no control over them or their journey. The separation of journeys sometimes looks ugly but that is just to ensure we clearly see the changed path. If both paths looked too pretty, we wouldn't know which way to go.
    I am one who wants to bring everyone along with me on my journey, especially if it is one I am excited about. I really

struggle with the people closest to me going in a different direction. It has taken me a long time to understand this and I still struggle to accept it but I have learned through my experiences that once I accept the change of path my road becomes smoother.

The best thing I can do for myself is to always show myself love and keep pushing through the tough times. Distractions can be sent our way to keep us from our destination. It takes too much time and energy to convince others to be like us. Not everyone is going to accept everything about the way we are and that's ok. It doesn't mean they will leave our lives, it just means they are not in this part of the journey with us. They can come back to our journey at any time. It all depends on their progress and when it crosses our path again.

Life is too short to focus any time on negativity. Just be a good person, flood your mind with positive thoughts, and surround yourself with like-minded people. This energy will bring in the right people and the people around you will be influenced by your energy. You do not want to be in a position to be influenced by their negative energy. The people who are meant to walk the same path as you will bring you more joy and you will be able to move along much faster.

When I am at a point where I am not sure if a person is coming or going in my life, I just focus on me and take a moment to be still. I do the things with which I am most comfortable and allow nature to take its course. I know who I am and where I am going in life.

Sometimes I have tried to follow a path to keep others happy. It is a very hard road to travel. They are the ones who end up happy while I am distracted and uncomfortable.

I hope the lessons I have learned on my journey are able to have a positive impact on you. Acceptance has been a huge step for me when heading in the right direction. If I keep the focus on me and show compassion to everyone I encounter, whether it be a positive or negative encounter the effects on me are almost always good. Remember the other person may be feeling the same loss as you because you are not following them on their path. Send them on their way with love so when you meet again there will be no hard feelings, only growth.

"Sometimes you don't see the millions of people who accept you for what you are. All you notice is the person who doesn't."

-Jodi Picoult

Life's Whispers

Chapter 8
My Beautiful Brie

The year was 2010 and we were newly certified foster parents. A baby girl had recently been placed with us. We were truly enjoying this new adventure and so were our three biological children. My daughter Natalia was the only girl, so for her to have a baby girl at home was the absolute most exciting thing. Liam just loved not being the baby. It made him feel instantly older. Michael was a teenager, and the baby took to him immediately.

The first week of May we received a call.

"Good Morning, Dawn. This is Mary, a social worker with the agency you are fostering through. I am calling to see if you have room for two girls for a weekend while their foster parents are on vacation?"

"I think so. I'll have to bring a set of bunks beds from my parents but we can make it work. Plus Natalia would be so excited to spend the weekend with them."

"Their names are Cathy and Nathaly, they are primarily Spanish speaking but they know enough

English for you to communicate with them."

"Ok, see you Friday."

When they arrived at our house it felt like they had just come home, as if they had always been there. Kathy walked into the bedroom we had set up for them, looked around, then with her eyes real big she said "I had a dream about this place a couple weeks ago." At the time I really didn't think much of it. I didn't believe she really had a dream about our house. I thought she was just saying it.

The kids played nonstop; we barely saw them. The first night they were at the house we went out to dinner and then the last day we had a Mother's Day gathering at our house. My mother and mother-in-law came to celebrate the day with us and our guests. We all sat out back on the deck, barbecued some food, enjoyed the warm sunshine and each other's company.

As the party was coming to an end a sense of sadness took over and nobody wanted to see the girls go back home but we all knew their foster parents would be coming to get them shortly. Kathy told me she had made a surprise for me and wanted to give it to me before she left. It was a letter.

Dear Dawn,

Dawn I like stay here for ever because you are a good mother, and because I want Liam and Natalia be my sister and brother and I want you to be my Mom and I like your family too because they are funny
and they are great persons

Happy Mothers Day.
Love, Cathy R."

After reading that I wasn't sure how I could ever let them go.

As I watched them walk out the door, I had a hollow feeling in my chest. Every muscle in my face dropped, I shook my head back and forth while rubbing my forehead. My mom watched me for a moment.

"Dawn, What can you do to get them back?

With a quavering voice I replied, "I don't know."

I had such an empty pit at the bottom of my stomach that wouldn't go away. Over the next few weeks, I reached out to the social workers several times to check on them. I also let the workers know if they were ever moved into permanent placement, we would love for them to come with us. I later found out athy had been bugging the social workers to come live with us.

At the time I was working in an emergency room. When I would have some down time late into the night I would go on my computer and search for them. I would intensely stare at the screen, tapping away at the keyboard while swinging my leg back and forth. My coworker would walk by and say, "Dawn are you ok? You look so serious."

"I'm ok, just looking up the two girls who stayed at our house for the weekend."

"You really miss them, don't you?" formatting issue here I can't seem to fox - tabs?

    I can't stop thinking about them. They're on my mind all the time. I know I won't find anything on here. I suppose I'm just looking for a way to connect with them. Maybe to make sure they're okay and to see if they are available for adoption. I feel like they belong with us."

The connection I felt to them was so strong. I thought of them all day long. I worried about how they were, how they were adjusting to school, and wondered if they were still thinking of us. I would even dream of them. I almost felt like I was going crazy. Was I obsessed with them? It wasn't just me though. Everyone in the house would ask about them and family would call asking if we had heard anything from them.

I found out Cathy and her sister were in foster care because they had been horribly abused. Cathy endured most of the abuse and it showed. She was very shy and scared but felt completely safe and protected when near my husband and my eldest son Michael. I assumed it would not be easy for them to find a home that she would be comfortable in. We never expected to take in more than one child and now we were thinking of taking two more on top of the baby we had already been placed with. That would total six children but everything seemed as though it what was meant to be.

In June, their foster mother called. "Dawn, would you and the family like to come to Cathy's school concert?"

"Yes, we would love to! We miss them so much."

"They miss you too."

The night of the show we all got dressed up and we were so excited. Butterflies danced in our stomachs. Cathy didn't know we would be there; they didn't want her to be too nervous on stage. When the show ended, we waited in the hall. As the double doors opened and she came out the whole place seemed to disappear as she spotted us in the crowd. Her face lit up, she stood tall and confidently walked toward us. It was just us and her. The connection was like no other. We had an unspoken, mutual understanding that she was part of our family. That summer we stayed in contact and celebrated Nathaly's 10th birthday together.

When we arrived at the party they had no idea we were coming. It was a hot July afternoon. We were taken right to the back yard. The sound of splashing and giggles were coming from the pool. I looked but did not see them. All of a sudden out of nowhere they came running up to us and gave us a big hug. They were both smiling ear to ear. Little did I know the next time I would see them after this visit would be when we were moving them into our home.

It felt like an eternity but really it was only a couple months. Sometimes people come into your life and you just know they are meant to be there. You can feel the magic deep in your soul. As if someone or something had their hand in orchestrating these events and you can feel that you were destined to be together.

So it was extremely painful when we lost Cathy, also known as Brielle after her adoption, to a sudden and unexpected illness just weeks after she gave birth to her beautiful baby girl. I could not accept that we were destined to be together and this was how her story would end. I knew there had to be more. There had to be a purpose for all of this.

I could not comprehend the idea of her being gone let alone the thought of her story just ending. Why would this connection be orchestrated just for her to be taken away. We were not a wealthy family. It's not like she was sent to us to have this extravagant life before she passed away. The only thing we had to offer was unconditional love.

I had this knowing feeling again in the pit of my

stomach. I asked myself over and over again "Why would this happen and my job as her mom can not be over." Life can't be that cruel. How could we be blessed with such a wonderful gift in life and then it just be ripped away from us leaving us completely broken and empty. There had to be a reason. I couldn't accept anything less.

At the same time I was wanting to document all our memories of her for us in a book for us all to remember her as she was. At some point our memories will eventually fade, and I couldn't bear the thought of forgetting anything about her. It became crippling knowing I only had so much time to get everything in writing and I had no one to write it all down for me.

A friend of mine kept telling me I was capable of doing it myself but I could not see it. I could barely help the kids with their homework. How could I write a book, even if it was only for us all to see. She kept insisting. "Just start writing. Write down anything that you can remember," she told me several times.

I started writing and when I had the first chapter completed, I contacted an editor. I figured she'd secretly be laughing at me and we would have a lot of work cut out for us but to my surprise she didn't. She treated me like I was an author. I never felt as though this was something I couldn't do. She guided me all the way through our beautiful story and helped me publish that book. With her guidance I accomplished way more than I ever expected.

I don't know what God's plan was in this journey but I have found a gift within myself that I never knew I had and I plan to continue sharing her story, our story to help others. I have many healing books within me that are working their way out. This is the only way I have found peace—dealing with the pain she experienced and the pain we will always experience missing her.

I never expected the book to be so healing for me as well as others, I really just wanted to make sure we always had her best memories at our fingertips. Life really has a wonderful way of bringing us comfort after such horrible pain if we are open to it and open to trying new things.

Brie's full story can be read in my book, *Picking Up the Pieces; My Journey with Grief, Greatness and God.*

Chapter 9
About Life's Whispers

Have you ever gotten a feeling deep in your gut and you just know something is right or wrong? Or someone pops in your head randomly and then a few days later you hear news about them? Or maybe you avoid going to a place and then realize it was better off that you didn't go there? These are what I call life's whispers.

They are there to direct you on the path you are most comfortable on. They are meant to be small reminders of the person you were born to be. The problem is, life happens and we get distracted and sometimes the whispers are so quiet we miss them or just don't recognize what they actually are.

I believe when I met Cathy for the first time, life was whispering in my ear. It was letting me know we were meant to be together. I knew our relationship was special but I had no idea how much of an impact it would have on me and my life. I never expected for a child to teach me so many life lessons. I am so glad I never gave up on my feelings because I would have missed out on some of the best memories of my life. It wasn't until after her passing that I started looking for answers.

At the time I knew nothing about life's whispers so I just thought I was thinking of her too much, and that something was wrong with me. I could not understand how life could be so cruel. I could not move forward in my life with the events that had happened. Why would I have such a strong connection to her but not get to spend my whole life with her? I just knew that life must have had a deeper purpose for us being together.

We experienced so much in such a short time. She did so much work on herself and I got to watch her blossom into this beautiful woman and mother. I could not even comprehend that she did all that work for nothing. As soon as she got to the good part of life she was taken away. It just made no sense to me.

During this time I was also getting that same gnawing feeling in my gut, but this time it was about writing a book. I started to wonder what was going on and I wanted the feeling to stop but didn't understand why it was happening. I knew from experience the feeling wasn't going to go away and was going to continue to get more intense until I addressed it.

Life's whispers can come disguised as crazy ideas. When I mentioned to my family and friends about writing a book some of them chuckled at me. I don't blame them. When I decided to go for it I chuckled at myself. Who was I to think I could write the book? But we will never know until we try, and that's exactly what I did.

I never gave up on my feelings and took a leap of faith. When I started to write the book, I could not see the road ahead. I just took the first step, and now that I have gotten through writing that book and have processed everything, I can look back and see that it was exactly what I was supposed to be doing. Maybe we went through all that so I could share our story with others and to let them know they are not alone. I do not believe in coincidences, and I know I would have never traveled to this destination without all that has happened.

Before my experiences in losing Brie, I had never written a book and never thought about it. I actually never wrote anything to speak of, or even had the desire. I wonder how many other things I could have experienced or done but because I didn't pay attention to the signs, I missed the opportunities. I am sure we all have those missed opportunities in our lives..

I now make sure that I pay attention to the way I feel in different situations. Especially ones where I feel very emotional. These feelings are all indicators of whether we should stay on the path we are currently traveling or stop and evaluate our situation.

I am committed to living my life to the fullest in memory of my daughter who was not given the same opportunity. I am forcing myself to never ignore these subtle signs. I must say since I decided to do this so many new opportunities have been brought to my attention.

I have met so many new people who have all helped me along my journey and I have no doubt this will continue to happen. I wake up excited to see where the day will take me. I now feel a purpose to my life where before I was just busy and always going, but I often had an emptiness inside me.

I hope that at least once in your lifetime you take a leap of faith and see what life in store for you.

What if the life you have planned for yourself is not as fulfilling as the life that is really out there waiting for you to claim?

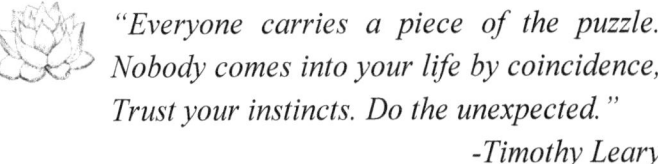
"Everyone carries a piece of the puzzle. Nobody comes into your life by coincidence, Trust your instincts. Do the unexpected."
　　　　　　　　　　　　　　　-Timothy Leary

The Third Law of Motion

Chapter 10
Candace

When it comes to my family, grocery shopping is always an adventure, and I have learned that anything can happen at any time. An outing with six kids is always unpredictable. It requires an expert level of multitasking. As I walk down the aisle, I am, at all times, trying to make sure all kids stay with me, remembering to get everything on my list, being aware of what the little ones are sneaking in the cart when they think I'm not paying attention, and making sure to keep an eye out on our surroundings. On any given day our local store is packed solid. There are often long lines, never enough checkout lanes open, and the aisles are packed with people and their shopping carts.

On this particular day things happened I never expected, but I believe God had a hand in my life and the life of an acquaintance. I was in the front aisle by the checkout lanes and I noticed an acquaintance, with whom I had gone to grade school. I made eye contact with her but she didn't seem to recognize me. I was glad she didn't recognize me. It can be hard to stop and have a conversation with someone while keeping six kids under control. Plus, I have a very limited time to shop before they start having meltdowns. I really didn't think much of it but wondered what she was up to. I thought to myself, "Is she waiting for someone or is in need of something?"

I had heard through the grapevine that she had several run-ins with the law and battled addiction. When I saw her she was not the happy vibrant girl I remembered. It appeared that life had not been so easy on her. I thought maybe the rumors were true. I remember saying to myself, "God Bless her." I was living comfortably but life had been rough on me too, just in different ways.

I continued shopping and really gave it no more thought. I did not see her the rest of the time I was there. As I stood in line I made a call to my eldest daughter who was walking around with the other children because they were getting bored with me. "Brie, can you guys come back with me? I am in lane four checking out."

"Okay, we are walking toward you now. Be there in a minute." she replied.

"Okay, see you soon."

As I stood in line loading my overloaded cart onto the conveyor belt, I saw the acquaintance coming toward me. She was pushing a cart with two littles ones sitting in the back. As she got closer I realized she was coming up right behind me. I turned toward her and said, "Hello." Her hands were fidgeting all over the place as she responded.

"Hey, can I ask you a question?"

"Sure, what is it?"

"I have a gift card for $100. If I use this gift card to pay toward your bill would you give me $80 cash. I won't take the money until the gift card has been approved and applied toward your bill."

I thought for a second; many scenarios played through my head. I knew none of them really mattered. I had the means to help her so why shouldn't I? There were really no good reasons not to. I never carry cash but that day I had exactly what she asked for. I replied, "Yes, I can do that for you." She looked shocked, as did the lady working the register. My acquaintance very happily replied, "Thank you!"

We stood quietly waiting for the cashier to ring everything up. I took out the $80 to show her I really had it with me. I didn't want her to think I was scamming her.

When Brie and the other children came back they kept looking at me with very unsure faces. After a few minutes standing there, Brie leaned in toward me and whispered, "Is everything ok?" I gave a comforting smile and nodded yes. Not one of the kids acted out or asked for all of the candy that was spread out along the checkout aisle. Their eyes were glued to our every movement, and they were engulfed in the silence.

I was not one bit worried that the gift card would go through. I had a feeling she had been standing at the front of the store asking many people but since she was still there, I assume everyone told her no. She would not put herself in this position if there was a possibility it wouldn't work but even if it didn't, I would just pay for the bill as I had already planned and we could go our separate ways. At this point I could still tell she had no idea who I was.

The last item was scanned. The cashier asked, "Do you have any coupons?"

"No" I replied.

"Your total is $428.64"

The girl I went to school with stepped forward with her $100 gift card and ran it through the payment system. I watched as it deducted the $100 from my bill. When she was done I thanked her for what she had done for me. The $20 discount on my groceries was huge for my family. With so many people in the house every penny counts.

She was then ready for me to fulfill my end of the deal. I firmly held the money in my hand as I raised it up. I made strong eye contact with her but she was not looking at my face. As she went to take the money I didn't let go, causing her to look directly into my eyes. I paused a moment before I said "Candace, I know you are going to do the right thing with this money."

When I said her name, her jaw dropped to the ground. I could tell she definitely had no idea who I was. She assumed I was a stranger and would have no one to tell. Possibly a moment of fear set in for her but either way her secret was safe with me. As she continued to look at me in wonder, I saw a light go on and she said "Dawn?"

"Yes, it's me."

"Oh. I'm not like that any more, and I have these little ones with me."

"It was nice seeing you, Candace. I hope you guys have a wonderful night."

I suspect the money I gave her was not used for the children in her cart but used to feed her addiction. That's okay though. It is not my role in this world to judge. I did what I was called to do that day and that's all that matters. Sometimes people who get caught in addiction no longer feel seen or heard. They walk around feeling invisible to others and their surroundings. No one should ever feel this way.

I was sure the eight sets of little eyes which gazed upon us that day, the two in her cart and the six with me, would remember that encounter in the future. I aspire to be a good role model for them and the people around me. I also hope the adults and other children in the store who happened to observe our encounter walked away with a different perspective too.

Thanks to social media I have been in continuous contact with her since then. It has been such a blessing to be able to watch her grow. I have seen her in and out of prison, get clean, hold a full-time job for several years, purchase her first new car, and get married and make many beautiful memories in her home with her family. I have never spoken to her about the events that took place that evening. I am not sure if it has had an impact on her but I hope I reminded her that her presence on this earth matters.

Chapter 11
About
the Third Law of Motion

None of us really know how the universe works. We have so many questions that have not been answered. Is there a God? Is there something bigger than us out there? Are we being watched? Are we being judged for our actions? Do we get back exactly what we put into the universe?

Can you imagine, if what we do has an impact on the things that the universe gives to us? The impact that could potentially affect our children and our family members could be profound. I am sure a lot of us would do things differently. I know without a doubt this would have an impact on my decision making.

I took a deep look in the mirror and asked myself, "Who do you want to be and what type of people do you want to be surrounded by?" Well, that answer was very easy for me. I always wanted to give service to the world in the most loving way possible and I want to be surrounded by like-minded people.

I believe when you are doing things with love it raises your vibration and attracts people who are at the same vibration level as you. Vibration creates a big circle around you full of the people who have an equal vibration frequency. This is true with low vibration levels too. When you find yourself surrounded by negative people it may be a good idea to evaluate how much energy you are putting into negative situations.

I always try to remind myself that my children are observing me and what I do will have an impact on them and then on their children and so on. My goal is to give them as many positive experiences as possible. This could turn into such a wonderful snowball effect. One person has the ability to change the world just by making one loving change.

I pray that if any of my children or grandchildren are out in the world struggling to be seen, that I have done everything in my power to offer them help. I also want to be a good example to them so they know the type of people to feel comfortable asking for help. There are so many good people in this world.

After what I would call too much thinking about the universe, an idea came to me. I was just sitting there and a light bulb turned on above my head just like in the cartoons. I should live my life as if that was true. It may not be true, but I see no reason not to do it. For myself I feel so much better when I do good things and I am not affected by other people's opinions of me and my actions.

Maybe it would only have a placebo effect on me, but I am okay with that because I see no reason for it not to have a positive impact on my life and the lives of others. But when you think about it, why wouldn't it be true? Newton's third law of motion states that every action has an equal and opposite reaction. It does not state "Universe not included."

It made perfect sense if I put out good, good will come back to me, and if I put out bad that's exactly what I will get in return. If it doesn't work out that way it's okay because I am doing these things with good intentions therefore I feel good about the things I am doing and the decisions I am making.

You may wonder, "What could anyone say bad about doing something good for another?" But they do and they will. When I helped out my friend, I felt so good about it. I went and told family and friends and I was shocked at their responses. "You know she took the money and bought drugs, right?" "Why would you do that?" "I would never do that."

I could not believe people would base what they did on someone else's actions. My friend was obviously struggling and needed someone. I don't know if she used the money for drugs. I do know that we made eye contact and I was kind to her, and she felt love. Love is so powerful I believe it tops negativity. Each day when entering they world and encountering others please do it with love.

 *"To love a person is to see all of their magic, and to remind them of it when they have forgotten."*

-Unknown

Kindness

Chapter 12
Francesca

"Bye Mom, I'll be back later." I yelled as I ran out the front door and hopped into my car. A few seconds later, as I was pulling out of the neighborhood a call came through and I hit the answer button on my steering wheel. "Hello, that was quick. I barely got out the door." I said, laughing.

"Where are you going in such a rush?" my mom said.

"Remember, I'm meeting a new friend tonight. I've never met her in person before."

"Oh my god, I forgot. Good luck and call me later." as soon as you're done. I want to hear all about it."

"Okay. I will but I gotta go so I can follow my GPS."

"Okay, bye."

"Bye."

When I walked into the restaurant I realized I had no idea who I was looking for. I only knew her name. Since I was a little early I decided to get us a table and I would continue to look for the most clueless person walking in the door. I'm sure that's how I looked walking in.

When I thought I saw her I stood up, walked over, and said "Francesca?"

"Yes" she replied softly. "I'm assuming you are Dawn?"

"Yes, I got us a table already. Follow me. I must say you look beautiful. Absolutely stunning."

"Thank you," she blushingly replied

We sat and talked about small things while we ordered our food and ate our appetizers. "So, what do you do for a living?" I asked.

"I worked as an EMT previously but currently I am working as a 911 operator. How about you?"

"Currently, I am a real estate agent. I too used to be an EMT. I didn't do it for long because it was too much for me because I was working at the hospital in the ER plus raising my kids."

Both of us shared a love of working in the medical field, the excitement and the reward felt by helping others. We both missed it but life had taken us down a different path. At that moment the waiter came with our food. As he placed my plate in front of me he said, "Excuse me, the plate is extremely hot. Please be careful."

"Thank you" I said.

Before he walked away he looked at us both and asked "Is there anything else you need? A refill?"

"No, I am good. Thank you," we both replied.

As he turned and walked away we heard a death curdling scream coming from the kitchen. We both looked up at one another. Our eyes locked. I don't remember a word being spoken but a full conversation was held between our eyes.

"Someone must have slipped and their arm went into the fryer," I thought to myself. I have no idea why that was my thought besides I knew it had to have been an extremely painful event due to the level of pain I could sense in the scream.

Since we had just ended that conversation we both knew what we needed to do and hopped up and started running towards the kitchen door. The manager would not let us back so Francesca raced out to her car and grabbed her medic bag. I stood with the manager and when Francesca returned the manager realized we had the means to help her employee. "I'm sorry I stopped you. I thought you just wanted to go back to look. I didn't realize you were able to help."

We pushed open the kitchen doors and standing in the back of the kitchen was a broken young man who had sliced his arm with a box cutter and a manager who had a look of panic. Blood was literally dripping down his arm and a female manager was desperately squeezing the area of the wound to stop the heavy flow of blood from coming out. She looked up at us and yelled "HELP!"

Francesca set down her bag, together we opened it, took out the supplies and she put on the gloves and headed over to assess the situation. "Dawn, I need the tourniquet STAT."

I grabbed it, started running toward them and we met in the middle. She grabbed it out of my hand and went right back over and applied the tourniquet to his arm. I then stood there and handed her the bandages and gauze as she wrapped it up. As I watched them I saw this beautiful person realizing their life was flashing before their eyes. When he would look over toward me I made sure to give him the most loving look, a look of compassion and comfort.

I could see his pain. He begged us to save him. He had instant regret. He did not want to die that day. He was just desperate for help. Desperate to be heard and desperate to be seen. We have all been in a place of struggle. We have all been in a place where we don't know how we'll make it through the struggle because it just seems like too much at the time. I can't even imagine how hard that decision had to have been on him. The pain I watched him experience both emotionally and physically was unbearable. I can't imagine the level of desperation it took to carry out that act.

I prayed for him at that moment. I asked God to please cover him with his love and to help him see all the resources available to him. I asked God to keep shining the light bright over him. He was given a second chance that day and I prayed he would find the answers as to why, what was his purpose in this life. Life can be so much easier when we find our purpose.

When the ambulance arrived, we both went to the bathroom, cleaned up and sat back down to our dinner. Neither one of us could believe what had just happened. The adrenaline was pumping through our veins.

It was evidently clear to us and everyone around us that we were meant to be there that day. Our conversations did exactly what they were supposed to do. It let us both know, together we could handle what was about to happen. We thought we were there on a date but in reality we were there to do our part in saving a young man's life. We were there to give him and the workers comfort while they waited for the EMS to arrive.

I can't help but believe there is something bigger than us out there. Some of the things I have encountered in my life are too much of a coincidence. This gives me comfort. I love knowing that the weight of the world is not all on me. I speak to whoever it is out there and ask them for help all the time.

Francesca and I only went on a date that one time but have kept in contact and have a very close friendship. We are forever bonded by that moment. I went back to the restaurant a few days later to check on the gentleman and left a gift basket for him. I have kept in contact with him via social media and love seeing how well he is doing. He looks incredibly happy.

I'm sure you can guess what I did as soon as the date was over. I got into my car and made a call...

"Mom, you'll never guess what happened...

Chapter 13
About Kindness

Could you imagine how different the world would be if we all made an effort to be kind to everyone we encountered? We get so caught up in our lives that we miss many opportunities to embrace casual encounters with others. We dance around the world surrounded by many, yet we are all alone. We are so engulfed by social media, our own thoughts, and the pressures life puts on us we don't even recognize that there are people around us.

That day at the restaurant the poor guy was surrounded by tons of people, but not one person recognized the pain he was in. The cooks were running around the kitchen, waitresses were back and forth between tables and kitchen, the cashiers were engaging with everyone who came in, not to mention all of the customers sitting at the tables. Yet not one person looked into his eyes and felt his pain.

When I saw him I had no doubt he did not want to die, he just did not want to live in emotional pain any longer. The stress life dishes out can be physically and mentally unbearable. We all need to slow down and realize none of it is going anywhere and we will be okay if we don't get it all done in one day.

Everyone goes through difficult times so everyone can relate to the need to be supported during those times. Everyone experiences their pain differently and for some it just becomes too much. They are the people who need love the most. The good thing is love has no limits. You can give it out all day long and you will never run out.

This topic is so personal for me because of my biological father's suicide. What if his event was a cry for help? Unfortunately his cry went unanswered and his attempt at suicide was successful. He did call 911 but by the time they got to him it was too late. I just can't help but think how many people are out there every day thinking about ending their life and no one ever notices.

This does not require a lot from any one person. If we all just gave a little more to the ones around us the world would be such a better place. We would feel better, and so would the other people around us. I am a strong believer that what one puts out is what they get in return. I can't think of anyone who would not want people to be kinder to them.

One good tip I have heard is that when people are talking to you about something they are going through, listen to them eighty percent of the time and only talk twenty of the time, and only two percent of the conversion should be about your own personal experiences. This way the other person feels a connection and feels that they are being heard. Being heard also gives a sense of validation and that is a huge step in processing through problems.

There is no need for judgement, opinions, or negative

comments. Life can naturally be difficult and there is no need to add to it. We are all doing our best with the life we have been given and your kindness may be the answer to that person's prayers.

If you know someone who has struggled or if you have struggled yourself, I ask you to do 1 small act of kindness each week for another injured soul and I ask you to try your best to be the kindest version of yourself.

"Ah, kindness. What a simple way to tell another struggling soul that there is love to be found in the world."

-Unknown

Failure

Chapter 14
Family Visit

It was a warm sunny May afternoon. We had been in our new house less than a year and our out-of-state family couldn't wait until the weather warmed up so they could come spend some time with us. We enjoyed every moment with them. So many wonderful memories had been made during their stay. I particularly enjoyed looking out our living room window and watching their little ones play in the yard. My children were getting older, and I missed watching a toddler running with their infectious smile and hearing the continuous giggle.

I was feeling a bit run down and decided while all the kids were in school, I would lie down and take a nap on the couch. Our house guests had gone out for the day, and it felt like it was the perfect way for me to spend my afternoon. I made a cup of hot tea and sat down with my feet up on the couch. As soon as I finished the tea, I lay my head down on the pillow and fell fast asleep.

I didn't sleep very long so I know I must have quickly gone into a dream state. I was pleasantly surprised when I saw my beautiful Brie standing there before me in my dream. I looked over at our front door and saw our dog Maggie sitting outside on the front steps. I then heard Brie say, "I'm sorry Mom." I thought to myself, "Is she saying that because the dog is outside? Is she referring to her passing and leaving us? Maybe it's about all the arguing we did when she was a teen?" I finally responded to her.

"Brie, what are you talking about—'I'm sorry?' You have nothing to be sorry for."

The dream abruptly ended, and I woke up in a panic. I stood straight up and started pacing back and forth in my living room. I heard dogs barking and looked out back. I saw nothing. How could a quick nap feel so wrong? I loved that I had gotten to see Brie, but this visit from her did not sit right with me and I didn't know why. My heart was pounding, and my thoughts were racing. I felt emotionally out of control. My phone rang and I couldn't have been happier.

I never told the caller what had happened. I wanted to forget about it. Her call was a great distraction for me. I can't even remember what we talked about, but the call lasted about twenty minutes. I decided since I was awake, and the kids would be getting home from school, I would drive to the path where they walked home and surprise them with a ride. I waited and waited for them but never saw them. I even called their phones with no response.

I then decided to run into the grocery store for trash bags on my way home. The trash had been overflowing and desperately needed to be taken out but we had used the last bag the night before. I tried calling them again when I was driving home from the store but still no answer. When I turned down our street and started to approach our house I saw them all standing out front.

    The looks on their faces told me something wasn't right. My one daughter started to run toward my car as I pulled in the driveway. I knew whatever was going on she needed me immediately. She doesn't run! I threw the car into park even though it was still halfway in the road. When I hopped out and started running toward her she yelled, "Mom, they are doing CPR on Denise." This was the daughter of our company. I threw my keys down and screamed "F****CK!"

    I couldn't even comprehend why that would be going on or what had just happened. I ran like I never knew I could. I never even felt my feet touch the ground. I flew over the fence without even knowing if I touched it, ran across the yard and over a seven-foot-high deck railing. It felt as though the angels from above just grabbed me and carried me right where I needed to go. I did everything in my power to fight for her and her family. That's all I could do.

    That night I waited to hear if my efforts made a difference. I prayed and prayed. I also asked everyone I knew to join me in prayer. I kept thinking back on the dream I had of Brie and thought someone up there in heaven or whatever it is out there in the universe had to have their hand in this. Maybe we would get to watch a miracle unfold. We had already been through so much, why would God call us to experience this pain too? Hadn't we already felt enough pain for a lifetime? I couldn't understand how it would unfold any other way. Life just can't be that awful.

    Why would I be woken up in such a manner if it was not to save her life? I kept going over the events that took place when I woke up and then heard the dogs barking. Did I miss something? Was she out there then and I didn't see her? Could

I have saved her before it was too late?

It is unreal the thoughts that come and go while waiting for such news. They are uncontrolled and make no sense. Not only was I experiencing this but so were my teen children. Why couldn't God and the universe protect them? They did nothing to deserve this. They were still deep in the path of grief from the passing of their own sister. I worried for them and their future.

When we finally got an update on what was going on we were completely broken to hear Denise was no longer with us. All efforts made that day were not enough to keep her here with her family. I wasn't really sure how to process all that had happened. Over the next few days I was on the verge of a breakdown. I could not stop thinking about Denise, her family, my family, and our beautiful Brie.

On my worst day I walked, crying my eyes out the whole way, to the fire department. I had hoped someone would be there and could sit and talk with me. I know they have a lot of experience processing traumatic events and hoped they could offer me help or resources to get help, but no one was there. I worked very hard getting myself back from that dark place, but I am stronger than I ever knew I could be.

At the time I felt like such a failure. Why didn't I see her out there? I should have protected my children more. I should have made them leave but I needed their help and when it was all done they told me they felt better knowing they helped and didn't just sit back and watch. Sometimes we are called to do things above and beyond what we believe we are capable of but once we get through the entire journey we can look back and realize how strong we really are.

Chapter 15
About Failure

    Do you think a person can have the feeling of failure even though they did not fail? How is that possible? It is. We do it more often than we realize. I never really thought about failure in this way until I found myself in an extreme situation that had a strong impact on me. I convinced myself I had failed even though I did everything right.

    I kept looking back on the events that took place and I began focusing on the wrong things. I replayed every second over and over again in my head making sure I did everything exactly the way it should be done. I questioned every little detail and this left me in a very bad place mentally.

    Every day was a struggle. The pain and guilt I carried took a toll on me. I gained weight, looked visibly sad, and had dark circles under my eyes. I was having such a hard time getting past this stage of the healing process, it took me approximately a year to make any progress. It wasn't until I realized I was focusing on the wrong things that I could move forward.

When I was called to help I did everything to the best of my ability so why did I feel so defeated? I thought I was there to save Denise, but after many conversations with myself processing the events, I realized I do not have any control over someone living or dying.

I came up with a couple questions to ask myself when I would think about that day.

1. What do you believe you were there to do?
I was there to show the world how much her life mattered. I was there to fight alongside her Mom with all my might and I was there to hug her Mom when she needed it. I was also there so my children were not alone.

2. Do you think you did it to the best of your ability?
I sure did. I am only human so I can not say I did everything perfectly but I did it to the best of my abilities and with love.

3. Would you do it again?
I would do it over and over and over again even knowing the outcome because I believe I was meant to be there that day.

4. What changes would you make?
I would not change anything I did because I had no control over the events that happened. I would talk to myself nicer after the events and I would show myself the same amount of love and support I showed her family that day and all the days following.

Experiencing the traumatic event caused my brain to go into overdrive. Because I was so weak and vulnerable it took control of me. Once I got my power back and remembered I can control my thoughts, life got so much easier. When the negative thoughts would come in I would interrupt them with positive affirmations about myself. Ones I knew to be true. I also started to show love to myself.

We get so busy with life and healing ourselves from life we forget to be kind to ourselves. I believe it is one of the most important things we can do. It really should be as natural as saying good morning to our loved ones, a smile to a neighbor, or brushing our teeth.

I look in the mirror and say "Good morning beautiful. You are going to conquer today like a champ. I know you are tired but you have what it takes and I am so proud of you. Keep going. Don't forget you have little eyes watching you. I can't wait to see what awesome things you do today. I love you!"

Life can really dish out the hard stuff and we need to make sure we are countering that within ourselves. It is our responsibility to make sure we receive an equal amount of positivity. The world is not balanced and from my own experiences the negativity can weigh so much more than the positive. I now make sure I balance it myself.

The process does not happen overnight and is a lot of work. It actually takes quite some time but if you think about how long the suffering has taken a toll on you and how hard that is, the work does not seem so bad and there is a light at the end of the tunnel which gives the strength to keep going.

The questions I ask myself in this chapter I use in all different types of situations to evaluate my thinking. It has helped me tremendously. You are more than welcome to use them, just remember when answering you are being kind to yourself. Remember not to make things bigger than they really are and be honest. I hope this helps you as much as it did me.

 *"It all begins and ends in your mind. What you give power to, has power over you, if you allow it"*

-Leon Brown

Service

The time I spent as a home health aid is one I will always treasure. I worked as an aide for many years and cherish the time I spent with my patients. I learned many lessons during this time and would like to share a couple short stories with you. These two stories changed the way I look at life. Enjoy...

Chapter 16
Claire

Beep, Beep, Beep my alarm clock sounded. I sat up in bed not really wanting to get up but I knew there were people out there who were depending on me. I quickly got myself ready and headed out the door. The sun was still rising as I drove through what looked like fallen clouds. I pulled in the driveway, knocked on the door, proceeded to open it and yelled in "Claire, It's Dawn. I'm here," as I walked in.

"I'm in the bedroom," she replied in her soft, frail voice.

As I walked in the bedroom I saw her thin, weak body lying there. I stood next to the bed looking down at her and said "Good morning." I reached my hand behind her back as I grabbed her legs and in one swift move put her in a sitting position on the edge of the bed.

"Okay, I'm going to make your breakfast and then I'll help you shower."

TAB? "Thank you," she replied.

I scrambled up some eggs, made some toast, poured a

glass of orange juice, and made a cup of hot tea. I placed it all on a tray and carried it into her. I sat with her every morning while she ate. We would talk about many different things. Anything from politics, my son, television shows, and so much more but she rarely talked about her life. I imagine the past may have been too painful since she had lost almost everybody from that time of her life.

"How's your son?" Claire asked.

"He's good. He just learned how to ride a bike without training wheels."

"That's great. You must be so proud of him. I always wanted to have children but wasn't able to have them," she said.

"I am definitely one proud Mama and I'm so sorry. I didn't know that. That must have been so hard on you."

"It was and we didn't have a lot of options like now."

"Did you ever look into adoption?" I asked. She put her head down and sat quietly for a moment before answering. I reached my hand out and she placed hers in mine. "Yes, I was in my late twenties when we applied to adopt and after a long review we were told we were too old and how it wouldn't be fair for the child since we were not expected to live a long life."

I couldn't believe it. She was so young at the time and I was there caring for her while she was in her mid-nineties. She would have been such a wonderful mom and she would have offered a child or children such a great life. Not to mention she would have been around for a very long time.

"Did you look into any other adoption agencies?"

With tears running down her cheeks she said "No, I wish I had but when they told me that I believed them and didn't want to leave a child without parents. When I got older and wiser and realized I shouldn't have listened to them but by then I was really at the point where I couldn't adopt."

"Oh Claire, This is truly heartbreaking." I said as I hugged her. Now I understood why she always asked about my son and enjoyed stories of him so much.

It was time to change the pace of our visit. I didn't want to leave her alone and sad. "Claire, I am going to clean up breakfast and then I will help you shower and tell you all about my son's trip to the park. She looked up with a big smile and said, "I can't wait."

When I left her house, I wondered to myself how many times have I been told no and I accepted it. I decided from that point on I was going to live my life completely going after all the things I wanted even if others couldn't see it happening for me. I could see the pain she carried all those years later and I knew I did not want to leave this world with that pain.

Chapter 17

Isabella

The one thing I have learned from my time with the elderly or the dying is they almost never seem to regret the things they did in life but they do carry regret for the things they didn't do.

Knock, knock.

I opened the door and yelled in "Isabella, I'm here."

"I'm in the living room and I'm hungry. Are you here to make dinner?" she asked

I chuckled as I replied, "I am. I'm also going to help you get ready for bed while I'm here."

When dinner was made I sat with her just like I did every other patient. This was a good time for them to just enjoy some company. Some people don't have someone there to talk to throughout the day so I know it's important to take the time to just sit with them. Isabella was a little bit on the grouchy side and was a little demanding, but I always enjoyed the stories of her children, grandchildren, and friends. She was a busy beaver in her day, always on the go and involved in lots of social events. This day she seemed a bit down.

"Are you ok?" I asked.

"Yes. I am ok."

"How are your children?"

"They are good. Are you married?" she asked.

"I am."

"Do you love him?"

"I do. Why do you ask?"

"I was married to my husband until he passed away in his 50's. He was a great man and a great father but I don't know if he was the one for me."

"Why do you say that? You always talk so fondly of him." I was sitting across the room but decided to move closer to her. I had a feeling the conversation was about to get emotional, and I wanted her to feel supported and to know I was listening.

"I dated a man when I was younger but my parents didn't like him. I thought he just abandoned me. I didn't know it at the time but he was calling and sending letters but my parents intercepted them. After a year or so of waiting for him to come back I finally went out on a few dates with another guy. He was really nice and my parents loved him. After a few months he asked me to marry him. I said yes but still thought of the other guy quite often.

The wedding was planned fairly quickly. When I was leaving the church after the rehearsal a car pulled up in front of my fiancé's car. I saw my ex-boyfriend get out. I walked right over to him. My fiancé kept his distance and let me handle the situation. I asked, "What are you doing here?"

"I came to ask you not to marry him."

"Why would I do that?"

"I tried so hard to get ahold of you. Your mom would tell me you would call me back but you never did."

"I'm sorry. I can't do that. The wedding is already planned. It's too late." I turned around and walked away heartbroken. I was so mad at my mom. I couldn't believe she could do something so awful. From that point on our relationship was never the same.

I never forgot him and always wondered how things would have been different. I would see him often around town and we both lost our spouses early, but we never ended up together. I really think he may have been the one for me."

"Oh Isabella, that has to be the saddest love story I ever heard. It sounds like a script for a movie."

Now I understood why she was always so cranky. I can't even imagine living my entire life carrying the weight of those events. I believe all people come into our lives for a reason. Sometimes it's just to teach us a lesson. Being that they never ended up together even when the opportunity was available to them both later in life tells me they were not meant to be together.

Her mom interrupting their relationship also interrupted the lessons she may have needed to learn from him, therefore she carried that burden her entire life. Knowing her story and the time her story took place I don't think there was much she could have done differently but I know I can live my life better from the lessons I learned from her. I will be sure to take control of my life and know that I am always one decision away from the life I want. I will take into consideration the opinions of others, but I now know the long term effects of my decisions.

Chapter 18
About Service

When I first started working as a home health aide I was so excited to help those in need. I had learned so much in my training and I felt I had so much to offer. I was young, vibrant, and ready to conquer the world. Helping others gives me a feeling of being needed and fulfilling a purpose in life.

I was so naive. I had no idea they were the ones who were going to help me. They were the strong ones. Their bodies may have been weak but they had experienced so much and had learned so many lessons in life. They knew so much about things that I knew nothing about. The opportunity for me to learn was endless.

They would share the most fascinating stories and they'd almost always tell me the lessons they learned from their experiences. Their stories gave me a new perspective on life. It's always changing. One thing they all would say was you need to learn to live in the moment and always appreciate what you have because before you know it things will be different, and some things may be gone.

I have learned more than I could ever have offered. This

has happened to me not only in home care but any time I have been giving service to others. I have met some of the kindest people and I have met some not so kind people, but I have come to realize they both have their reasons why they are the way they are, and I am in no position to judge. I did not walk their path and I can only reference my own experiences. The only thing I can do is to make the time I have with them enjoyable.

I also believe when you give your time to others the universe notices and opens doors for you. Opportunities just start to open up and people come along your way with offers that you never expected. The universe is like anything else. It likes balance and positive interactions. The more positive we put out into the world the more positive we will get back and I think when we are in need and are someone who gives the universe will answer our prayers.

 *"It's your road, and yours alone. Others may walk it with you, but no one can walk it for you."*
-Rumi

Conclusion

Chapter 19
Grow with me

A few years ago when all the things in my life started to pile up on top of me, my burdens became too heavy for me to carry. I reached out to many people, listened to podcasts, and read books. They all pointed me in the same direction. I needed to go with it. Can you imagine? That's all I needed to do. I had all the answers but just didn't realize it.

The first step I took was recognizing what triggered me and looking into my past. This gave me great insight into what I needed to heal within me. It took quite a while and was very frustrating, but it has been worth it. I now take time to reflect on myself often so I do not get myself in this situation again. Meditation is something I never thought I was capable of because my brain never shuts off. Magically it has helped slow down my thoughts too. I make sure I go out often and enjoy the outdoors as the sun, water, and air bring me much joy. I take time to be with the people who are in front of me instead of on my phone.

We all carry this same power within. I wish someone had

told me sooner. Although honestly at times I may not have been ready to hear it because I was too focused on my feelings being validated by others. Little did I know I was the only one who needed to validate the feelings in order for me to heal and move forward.

Take the good and be grateful for every minute of it and when you come across negativity remember to take time to learn the lessons. Gratitude and lessons learned are the perfect recipe for growth. I hope these lessons I shared with you offered some help. I look forward to sharing more adventures with you all while we grow together.

 *"The final stage of healing is using what happens to you to help other people."*
-Gloria Steinem

Acknowledgements

Once again I am thankful for my friend and author R. C. McMenamin for seeing something in me that I never saw in myself. Without your encouragement I may never have found this talent.

Your belief in me has opened doors I may never have come across and met some of the most amazing people who I would have no other reason to connect with. I will forever be grateful to you. God and Brie: Thank you for sticking with me and guiding me on yet another path I would never have traveled alone. You guys are my rock. I give thanks to two wonderful ladies: Karen Hodges Miller and Lisa B. Snyder. You both are so wonderful, and I appreciate your patience and encouragement. Karen, thank you for always believing in me even when I am unsure, this is a quality not everyone gives out so freely. Thank you to everyone in my short stories. The impact you have had on my life has been profound and had given me the tools to help others in a positive way. Thank you to everyone who read the first book and now followed me on to the second. Your support is priceless.

About the Author

Dawn Ruggie is the mother to six beautiful children and grandmother to one little blessing. She is lucky enough to say that three of her children came to her and her husband through the foster care system.

Dawn has worked most of her adult life in the healthcare setting. In 2017 she became a real estate agent and absolutely loves it.

"I have had a wild ride in this thing we call life," says Dawn. "I decided to share my transparent and inspiring stories. I did not believe I was capable of writing a book but I went out of my comfort zone and trusted the advice of a good friend. I am happy to say I absolutely love it and am looking forward to writing many more."

www.ingramcontent.com/pod-product-compliance
Lightning Source LLC
Chambersburg PA
CBHW050304120526
44590CB00016B/2484